Seven Wonders of the
ROCKY PLANETS
AND THEIR MOONS

Ron Miller

TWENTY-FIRST CENTURY BOOKS

Minneapolis

To Lucas Liebermann

Photo Acknowledgments

The images in this book are used with the permission of: © Ron Miller, pp. 5, 7, 14, 16, 17, 25, 26, 28, 30, 32 (left), 33, 35, 39, 40, 42–43, 44, 45, 51, 53, 54, 56, 60, 61; NASA/JPL/USGS, pp. 6, 12, 18–19, 29, 75 (top right, bottom middle and right); © Karl_kanal/Dreamstime.com, p. 8; © Satellite Aerial Images/Universal Images Group/Collection Mix: Subjects/Getty Images, p. 9; NASA/Goddard Space Flight Center/Scientific Visualization Studio, p. 10; © Science Source/Photo Researchers, Inc., p. 11 (top); NASA/JPL/MSSS, p. 11 (bottom left); NASA/JPL, pp. 11 (bottom right), 37, 41, 75 (middle right and bottom left); © European Space Agency, p. 21 (top); © Adeliepenguin/Dreamstime.com, p. 21 (bottom left); © Martin Jakobsson/Photo Researchers, Inc., p. 21 (bottom right); NASA/GSFC/JPL, p. 23; © Tudorica Alexandru/Dreamstime.com, p. 24; © Gary Hincks/Photo Researchers, Inc., p. 27; © RIA Novosti/Photo Researchers, Inc., p. 31 (top); AP Photo, p. 31 (bottom); NASA/JSC, p. 32 (right); © Mauritius/SuperStock, p. 34; Library of Congress p. 46 (top, LC-DIG-hec-21052); NASA/JPL-Caltech/University of Arizona, pp. 46 (bottom), 47 (both); © Detlev van Ravenswaay/Photo Researchers, Inc., p. 49; © Apic/Hulton Archive/Getty Images, p. 50; NASA/Johns Hopkins University Applied Physics Laboratory/Carnegie Institution of Washington, pp. 52, 55, 57, 59; © Christian Darkin/Photo Researchers, Inc., p. 58; © Saiva/Dreamstime.com, p. 63 (top left); © Peter Kirschner/Dreamstime.com, p. 63 (top right); © David B. Fleetham/Photolibrary/Getty Images, p. 63 (bottom); © Dr. Jeremy Burgess/Photo Researchers, Inc., p. 64; © Science Faction/SuperStock, p. 65 (top); © Comstock Images, p. 65 (bottom); © Luis Fernandez/Dreamstime.com, p. 66; © Zafer Kizilkaya/Photo Researchers, Inc., p. 67; © Iulia Ioana Huiduc/Dreamstime.com, p. 68; National Park Service Photo by JR Douglass, p. 69; OAR/National Undersea Research Program (NURP); NOAA, p. 70; © Jasper James/The Image Bank/Getty Images, p. 72; © Pierre Mion/National Geographic/Getty Images, p. 75 (top left); © David A. Hardy/Photo Researchers, Inc., p. 75 (top middle).

Front cover: NASA/JPL/USGS (top left and middle, bottom right); © Pierre Mion/National Geographic/Getty Images (top right); NASA/JPL (middle and bottom middle); © David A. Hardy/Photo Researchers, Inc. (bottom left).

Twenty-First Century Books
A division of Lerner Publishing Group, Inc.
241 First Avenue North
Minneapolis, MN 55401 U.S.A.

Website address: www.lernerbooks.com

Library of Congress Cataloging-in-Publication Data

Miller, Ron, 1947–
    Seven wonders of the rocky planets and their moons / by Ron Miller.
      p.   cm. — (Seven wonders)
    Includes bibliographical references and index.
    ISBN 978–0–7613–5448–2 (lib. bdg. : alk. paper)
    1. Inner planets—Juvenile literature. I. Title.
  QB606.M55 2011
  523.4–dc22   2010015553

Manufactured in the United States of America
1 – DP – 12/31/10

Contents

INTRODUCTION

*P*EOPLE LOVE TO MAKE LISTS OF THE BIGGEST AND THE BEST. ALMOST TWENTY-FIVE HUNDRED YEARS AGO, A GREEK WRITER NAMED HERODOTUS MADE A LIST OF THE MOST AWESOME THINGS EVER BUILT BY PEOPLE. THE LIST INCLUDED BUILDINGS, STATUES, AND OTHER OBJECTS THAT WERE LARGE, WONDROUS, AND IMPRESSIVE. LATER, OTHER WRITERS ADDED NEW ITEMS TO THE LIST. WRITERS EVENTUALLY AGREED ON A FINAL LIST. IT WAS CALLED THE SEVEN WONDERS OF THE ANCIENT WORLD.

The list became so famous that people began imitating it. They made other lists of wonders. They listed the Seven Wonders of the Modern World and the Seven Wonders of the Middle Ages. People even made lists of undersea wonders and the wonders of science and technology.

But Earth isn't the only place with wonders. Our planet circles the Sun along with many other worlds.

WHAT ARE THE ROCKY PLANETS?

Three kinds of planets orbit the Sun. One kind is the rocky planets, such as Earth, Venus, Mars, and Mercury. These planets have a crust, an outer layer, made of silicate rocks. It is this kind of rock that gives the

This illustration shows the planets and their moons. The rocky planets—Mars, Earth, Venus, and Mercury—are the four small planets closest to the Sun. Earth's Moon is also visible in this illustration.

rocky planets their name. The second are the gas giant planets. These are planets made mostly of gas and liquid. They are Jupiter, Saturn, Uranus, and Neptune. Some astronomers, scientists who study the moon, the stars, and other aspects of space, call the icy world of Pluto a third kind of planet.

The rocky planets are made mostly of stone and metal. Earth, for example, has an outer crust, or a shell, of mostly rock and an inner core of mostly iron and nickel. The other rocky planets are similar. They hold deep canyons, tall mountains, poisonous skies, and the magic of life. Wonders can be found on every one of them.

OLYMPUS *Mons*

This image of the surface of Mars shows the largest volcano in the solar system—Olympus Mons.

$\mathcal{T}$HE SOLAR SYSTEM CONTAINS SOME HUGE MOUNTAINS. MOST ARE FOUND ON THE ROCKY PLANETS. THE GREATEST MOUNTAIN OF THEM ALL IS OLYMPUS MONS, A VOLCANO ON THE PLANET MARS. A VOLCANO IS A MOUNTAIN CREATED BY THE ERUPTION OF MOLTEN ROCK OR LAVA FROM WITHIN THE PLANET OR A MOON. *OLYMPUS MONS* IS LATIN FOR "MOUNT OLYMPUS." MOUNT OLYMPUS WAS THE HOME OF THE GODS IN GREEK MYTHOLOGY.

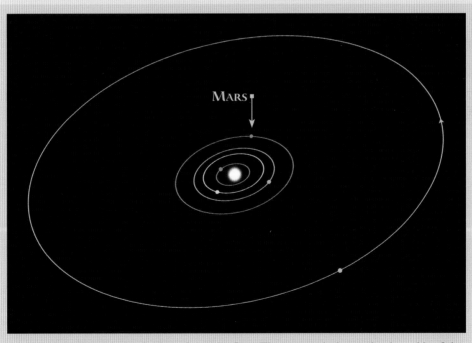

Mars is the rocky planet farthest from the Sun. The green circle marks the orbit of the first of the gas giants—Jupiter.

Earth's Mountains

Mount Everest is the highest mountain on Earth. It sits on the border between Nepal and Tibet, to the north of India. The peak of Mount Everest is 5.5 miles, or 29,029 feet (8.9 kilometers), above sea level. Humans exploring it often have to carry oxygen with them. The air at that height does not have enough oxygen in it for people to breathe easily.

The biggest mountain on Earth, however, is located in the middle of the Pacific Ocean. It is a volcano called Mauna Loa, part of the island of Hawaii. The whole island is really a big volcanic mountain rising from the ocean floor. Mauna Kea is the mountain's tallest peak.

Mount Everest reaches the highest point on Earth—more than 5 miles (8 km) above sea level.

This satellite image shows the Big Island of Hawaii. It contains both Mauna Kea and Mauna Loa, the tallest and biggest mountains on Earth.

At first glance, Mauna Kea may not seem like a very tall mountain. It is only about 13,800 feet (4,205 meters) above sea level. This is 16,000 feet (4,875 m) lower than the peak of Mount Everest. Most of Mauna Kea is underwater though. Measured from its base on the seafloor, Mauna Kea is actually more than 32,000 feet (9,750 m) high. Measured from base to peak, Mauna Loa is by far the tallest mountain. Another of Hawaii's mountains, Mauna Loa, is the largest mountain on Earth. Its base is more than 90 miles (145 km) across. It contains almost 20,000 cubic miles (80,000 cu. km) of material. This is twenty times the size of Mount Everest. Mauna Loa is so big and heavy that the mountain has actually bent Earth's crust beneath it.

GIANT OLYMPUS MONS

But as big as these mountains are, Olympus Mons dwarfs them both. It is fifteen times more massive than Mauna Loa. Its summit soars an unbelievable 17 miles (27 km) above the surrounding plains. This is three times higher than Mount Everest. Its base is 342 miles (550 km) across. On Earth, Olympus Mons would entirely cover the state of Missouri.

This false color image uses color to show the different elevations on the Martian surface. Olympus Mons is the large silver area.

During the four hundred years since 1610, when astronomers first studied Mars through telescopes, no one suspected that Mars had such a huge mountain. Astronomers thought that Mars was a much older world than Earth. They thought that if it had ever had high mountains, they would have long ago eroded (worn down by wind and water). They expected Mars to be a world of flat, dusty deserts with a few low, rolling hills.

In 1971 the *Mariner 9* spacecraft went into orbit around (circled) Mars. It took the first good close-up photos of the planet. Scientists were disappointed by these first pictures. The clouds of a vast dust storm buried the surface of Mars. The planet looked as featureless as a tennis ball. Then scientists noticed four dark spots in the blank cloud cover. They realized that the spots must be the tops of vast mountains. To rise above the dust cloud, these mountains had to be higher than any others then known in the entire solar system. Hints of craters in the centers of the spots suggested that all four mountains might be enormous volcanoes.

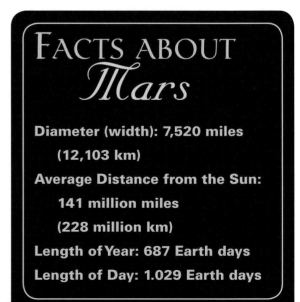

FACTS ABOUT
Mars

Diameter (width): 7,520 miles
   (12,103 km)
Average Distance from the Sun:
   141 million miles
   (228 million km)
Length of Year: 687 Earth days
Length of Day: 1.029 Earth days

The Mountains *That Weren't There*

Astronomers thought that if Mars had mountains, they would likely have snow on their peaks, just as the highest mountains on Earth do. The snow would look like tiny bright spots through the astronomers' telescopes. Sure enough, astronomers discovered several small bright spots near the south pole of Mars. These spots appeared in the same place year after year, so astronomers thought that they were the tops of mountains. They named them the Mountains of Mitchel *(below)* after Ormsby Mitchel, the astronomer who first saw them in the first half of the nineteenth century.

But when the first space probes visited Mars, they found no mountains at the south pole. The famous Mountains of Mitchel turned out to be large patches of white frost that appear every year in the same place.

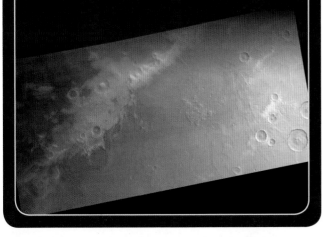

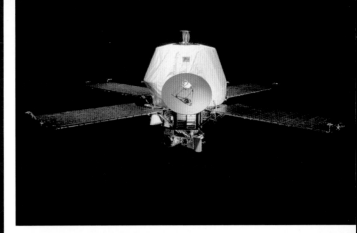

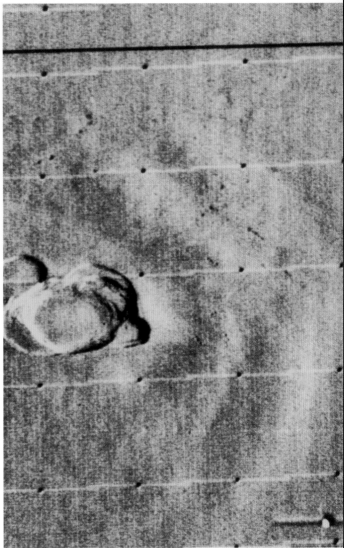

Top: Mariner 9 *was the first spacecraft to take good close-up photos of Mars.*
Bottom: *This Mariner 9 photograph from 1971 shows Olympus Mons standing above a dust storm on the Martian surface.*

> *"Olympus Mons is so big it would be impossible for an astronaut to see it from the surface of Mars. . . . It would be like trying to see the entire Rocky Mountain chain or the Great Lakes from one spot on the ground."*
>
> —William K. Hartmann, American astronomer, 2003

Once the dust settled, the probe took better photos. Astronomers realized that they had been right. The four mountains were huge volcanoes. They were the biggest mountains of any kind in the solar system.

HOW THEY CAME TO BE

Olympus Mons and its neighboring volcanoes are fairly young compared to the rest of the surface of Mars. They are about 1 to 3 billion years old. The volcanoes sit atop the Tharsis Bulge. This is a vast bulge on the surface of Mars.

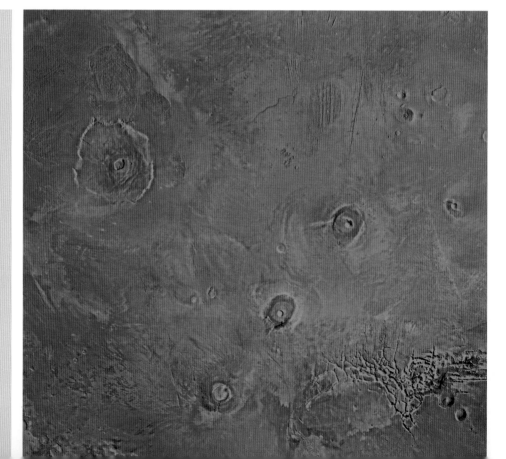

Olympus Mons (upper left) lies on the left of the Tharsis Bulge. On the right side of the Tharsis Bulge lie three more large volcanoes.

It is about 6 miles (10 km) high and about 5,000 miles (8,000 km) wide. Although the bulge is huge, you would never notice it if you were standing on it. It is almost one thousand times wider than it is high, so the angle of its slope is very small.

The Tharsis Bulge covers one-quarter of the Martian surface. A huge column of molten rock beneath the surface pressed on the crust of the planet to create the bulge. Similar places on Earth are called hot spots. The country of Iceland sits above one of these. Yellowstone National Park in Wyoming sits above another. The Hawaiian Islands form from another hot spot on Earth. Volcanoes have formed above these hot spots on Earth just as they have on the Tharsis Bulge. The hot spot on Mars may have cooled millions of years ago. The volcanoes above it may no longer be erupting lava.

The volcanoes on Mars are much bigger than those on Earth. Earth's crust is made of many stiff, rocky plates. These are like rafts drifting on the softer hot material that lies beneath. Mars's crust doesn't have separate plates. Its crust is much more rigid than Earth's. The crust of Mars can crack and shift, but it cannot float and drift the way the plates on Earth do.

Because Mars does not have a moving crust, its volcanoes tend to sit on top of their hot spots forever. This means that lava and ash just kept pouring out, building up layer after layer. This is why Olympus Mons is nearly two and a half times taller than Mauna Loa and many times wider and more massive.

Hot *Spots*

On Earth, hot spots tend to stay in one place while the surface crust moves above them. So a volcano will stay active only as long as it stays above its hot spot. If the crust moves it away from the heat, the volcano will cool. The chain of volcanoes that form the Hawaiian Islands is the result of the crust moving over a single hot spot. As the crust moves, a new volcano forms and its lava creates an island. Currently, the island of Hawaii is over the hot spot. Eventually, the island will move away from the hot spot and the volcano will slowly die. It will join the other extinct volcanoes in the island chain. Meanwhile, a new volcano will take its place. One is already beginning to form just off Hawaii's eastern coast.

"I have been watching and drawing the surface of Mars. It is wonderfully full of detail. There is certainly no question about there being mountains and large greatly elevated plateaus."

—Edward E. Barnard, American astronomer, 1894

This illustration shows an artist's idea of what the landscape of Mars might look like if someone were to stand on the rim of the giant caldera (crater) of Olympus Mons.

THE *Caldera*

The summit, or top, of Olympus Mons has a huge crater. It is a kind of crater called a caldera. A caldera is created by an explosion of gas and lava from the peak of a volcano. It can also form when lava drains out from under a peak. Either of these actions creates a huge cavity, and the top of the mountain falls into it. Crater Lake in Oregon and much of Yellowstone Park in Wyoming are calderas.

The Olympus Mons caldera is 50 miles (80 km) wide and more than 370 miles (600 km) around. This is about the same size as all of Yellowstone Park. The flat floor of the caldera is surrounded by steep cliffs that average nearly 2 miles (3 km) high.

VISITING OLYMPUS MONS

Olympus Mons is surrounded by cliffs up to 4 miles (6 km) high. Ancient glaciers, vast rivers of ice, may have made these cliffs. As the ice of the glacier flowed around the base of the mountain, it carved away the sides of it into high cliffs. A visitor to Mars would have to scale these cliffs before starting the journey up the volcano.

Strangely enough, once you reached the slopes of this tallest mountain in the solar system, you would hardly notice it. Even though the mountain is very high, it is also very wide. Its slope is less than one-third as steep as a typical wheelchair ramp.

Once you reach the highest point on the crater rim, you would be able to see for nearly 150 miles (240 km). But you would not be able to see the edge of the cliff you had climbed. The volcano is so wide that the cliff would be hidden below the distant horizon.

Olympus Mons will surely be one of the first stops for future tourists. Someday, visitors may be able to look out across it through a window in their Martian hotel!

2 VALLES Marineris

This illustration a shows future explorer looking across the vast expanse of Valles Marineris on Mars.

$\mathcal{J}$UST TO THE EAST OF THE GREAT VOLCANOES

OF MARS IS A SYSTEM OF CANYONS CALLED VALLES MARINERIS. THIS

NAME MEANS "MARINER VALLEY." THEY WERE NAMED AFTER THE

MARINER 9 SPACECRAFT, WHICH FIRST PHOTOGRAPHED THEM. THESE

VALLEYS ARE THE BIGGEST CANYONS IN THE SOLAR SYSTEM.

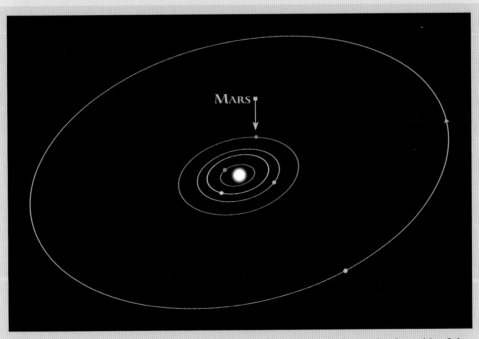

Mars is the rocky planet farthest from the Sun. The green circle marks the orbit of the first of the gas giants—Jupiter.

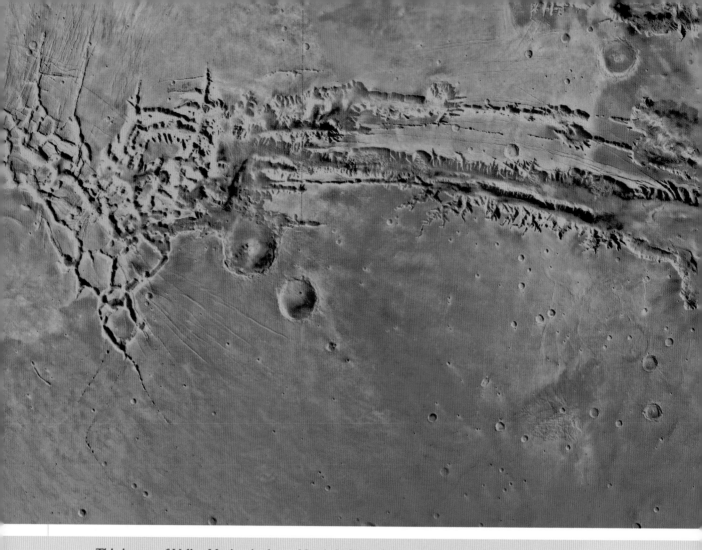

This image of Valles Marineris shows Noctis Labyrinthus and the full length of the 2,500-mile (4,0000 km) canyon.

Valles Marineris begins as a complex of canyons and valleys called Noctis Labyrinthus (Labyrinth of the Night). This system becomes a huge canyon. The canyon is so wide that if you were to stand on one rim, along most of it, you would not be able to see the opposite side.

With a depth of up to 3 to 4 miles (5 to 6 km), this canyon is about four times deeper than Earth's Grand Canyon. The Grand Canyon stretches across the northwestern corner of Arizona for 280 miles (450 km). Valles Marineris is 2,500 miles (4,000 km) long. If it were on Earth, it would stretch nearly across the United States. As Mars rotates, or turns around, one end of Valles Marineris has moved well into night while the other end is still in daylight. This could cause great differences in temperature from one end of the canyon

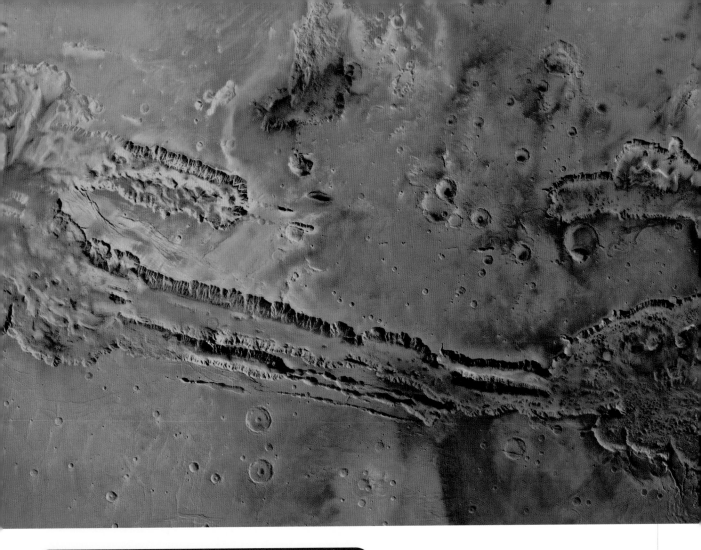

WHY IS Mars Red?

The most striking feature of Mars is its red color. Everything about the planet is red. The rocks are red, the sand dunes are red, even the sky is salmon pink. Mars is red because it is rusting. The soil on Mars contains large amounts of iron-rich minerals. The iron has combined with oxygen to form iron oxides, which are a reddish color. If you have ever seen a rusty piece of iron or steel, you have seen iron oxide.

to the other. The temperature differences would create powerful winds that would tear down the length of the canyon.

RIFT VALLEYS

It is not really fair to compare Valles Marineris to the Grand Canyon. The Grand Canyon was carved by running water. Valles Marineris was created when huge blocks of the Martian crust pulled apart. Mars does not have plates like those of Earth. Still, Mars's crust can move, shift, and crack. Many millions of years ago, the canyon was just a crack in the planet's surface. As the crust of Mars shifted, the crack opened and the walls spread apart.

Valles Marineris can be more accurately compared to Earth's Red Sea in the Middle East or the Atlantic Ocean. These enormous cracks in Earth's crust are called rift valleys. The valley of the Atlantic Ocean runs in a long S-curve nearly from pole to pole. Valles Marineris may look the way the Atlantic Ocean did more than 100 million years ago. A new rift valley runs down the center of the Atlantic Ocean. It is called the Mid-Atlantic Ridge. Valles Marineris also has a central ridge. Both ridges are caused by fresh rock rising from below as the crusts move apart. Forces other than movement of the crust have shaped much of the present-day Valles Marineris. Landslides and erosion—by wind and perhaps even by water—have made Valles Marineris the grandest canyon of all.

THE CANALS of Mars

In 1877 an Italian astronomer named Giovanni Schiaparelli announced that he'd seen thin lines crisscrossing the surface of Mars. He called these lines *canali*. In Italian this simply means "channels" or "grooves." English-speaking people mistook the word to mean *canal*. An amateur U.S. astronomer named Percival Lowell was sure that the lines were real canals, created by Martian engineers. Their purpose, he said, was to carry water from Mars's polar ice caps to the dry deserts farther south. A debate about the canals raged around the world. But astronomers had to wait until the first space probes took close-up photos of Mars.

When a probe finally arrived in 1969, the photos sent back to Earth showed not a single canal. But one feature on Mars did line up with one of Lowell's canals. That was Valles Marineris, the giant, 2,500-mile-long (4,000 km) Martian canyon.

"The Grand Canyon of Earth would be only a tributary [side] canyon to the grand canyon of Mars."

—William K. Hartmann, American astronomer, 1974

Above: *The deep channels of Noctis Labyrinthus are shown in this digital terrain model.*
Below left: *Earth's Grand Canyon is small compared to Valles Marineris.*
Below right: *The Mid-Atlantic Ridge lies under the Atlantic Ocean.*

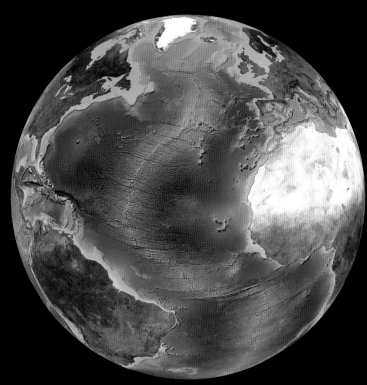

A GREAT VALLEY ON THE MOON

Earth's Moon has many great canyons too. The most famous is the great Alpine Valley. It splits an entire mountain range in half. The valley is 103 miles (166 km) long and more than 6 miles (10 km) wide. Alpine Valley was created when the surface of the Moon split along a fissure or crack in the surface. The two sides pulled apart, leaving the deep valley between. Lava flooded the floor of the valley. When it cooled and hardened, it created a hard, flat surface. Running down the middle of the flat valley is a narrow winding channel called a rille. The rille was originally a lava tube. This is a kind of tunnel through which lava once flowed. After the lava drained away, the top of the tube collapsed to create the rille.

GREAT VALLEYS ON OTHER WORLDS

The moons of other planets have valleys too. Messina Chasma on Uranus's moon

WATER ON *Mars*

Mars has many large channels that could have been formed only by the release of a huge amount of water in a short period of time.

The largest flood known on Earth occurred in the state of Washington about ten thousand years ago when a huge ice dam on a river burst and released a 1,000-foot (300 m) wall of water that roared across the landscape at 386 million cubic feet (11,000,000 cu. m) per second. The land downstream from this flood—called the Scablands—is similar to the land that appears downstream in the Martian channels. Some of the Martian floods were one hundred times larger than the one in Washington!

Some of the channels to the east of the Valles Marineris seem to have been created when an ice dam suddenly collapsed. Other channels appear in regions where the ground seems to have collapsed. When underground ice melted, the meltwater flowed away, and the ground above caved in.

Many scientists believe that water may have remained on Mars as underground ice. It is similar to the permanent layer of ice called permafrost that lies beneath the soil of Alaska and northern Canada. At the equator on Mars (an imaginary line around a planet), the ice may be 0.6 to 2 miles (1 to 3 km) thick.

Titania is one. It is a rift valley more than 0.5 miles (1 km) deep and almost 1,000 miles (1,600 km) long. It wraps almost one-fifth of the way around the small moon. An even bigger rift valley splits the surface of one of Saturn's moons, Tethys. Ithaca Chasma is more than 1,200 miles (2,000 km) long, 60 miles (100 km) wide, and from 2 to 3 miles (3 to 5 km) deep. This would be vast on any world, but on tiny Tethys, which is only 2,066 miles (3,328 km) around, Ithaca is a huge canyon. A canyon of the same proportions on Earth would stretch from San Francisco east all the way through Europe and Asia to Japan.

These rift valleys are all impressive. But for sheer spectacle, Valles Marineris tops them all. It is truly a wonder of the rocky worlds of the Sun.

The Valles Marineris cuts deep into the surface of Mars.

3 EARTH'S *Moon*

The Moon orbits more than 1,000 miles (1,600 km) from Earth.

$\mathcal{E}$ARTH'S MOON IS BIG. IT'S NOT THE LARGEST MOON IN THE SOLAR SYSTEM. JUPITER'S MOONS GANYMEDE, CALLISTO, AND IO AND SATURN'S MOON TITAN ARE ALL LARGER. BUT EARTH'S MOON IS HUGE COMPARED TO EARTH. JUPITER IS TWENTY-SEVEN TIMES LARGER THAN ITS LARGEST MOON, GANYMEDE. BUT EARTH IS ONLY FOUR TIMES LARGER THAN THE MOON. IF THE MOON WERE ORBITING THE SUN ON ITS OWN, IT WOULD BE A FAIRLY SIZABLE PLANET. IT IS ABOUT HALF THE SIZE OF MARS AND ONLY SLIGHTLY SMALLER THAN MERCURY.

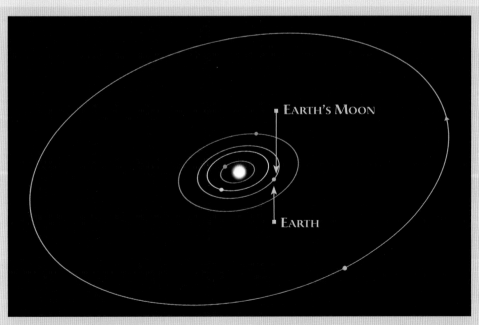

Earth, with its large moon, orbits between Venus (yellow circle) and Mars (red circle).

THE DOUBLE PLANET

Many astronomers have described Earth and its Moon as a double planet. The two bodies are certainly much closer in size than any other planet-moon combination. And both are made of the same kinds of rocks and minerals. This is because the Moon was created from material blown off Earth more than 4 billion years ago.

Billions of years ago, the solar system was still settling down after its creation. Thousands of bodies, large and small, zipped about every which way. They often collided into one another. The crashes created the many giant craters found on Earth, the Moon, Mars, and other worlds. Some of these bodies were as large as Mercury or Mars. One of these very large bodies crashed into Earth. Astronomers have even given it a name: Theia.

This illustration shows the comparative sizes of Earth and its Moon.

This computer artwork shows Theia colliding with Earth. The resulting material is believed to have come together to form the Moon.

When Theia collided with Earth, a huge amount of material was thrown into space. This material formed a ring around our planet. The material in the ring eventually came together to form the Moon.

Astronomers have another reason for seeing Earth and the Moon as a double planet. The Moon doesn't really orbit Earth. Instead, together the two bodies orbit a point between them. This common point is called the barycenter. The barycenter lies about 2,880 miles (4,640 km) from the center of Earth. That's still about 1,070 miles (1,710 km) from Earth's surface.

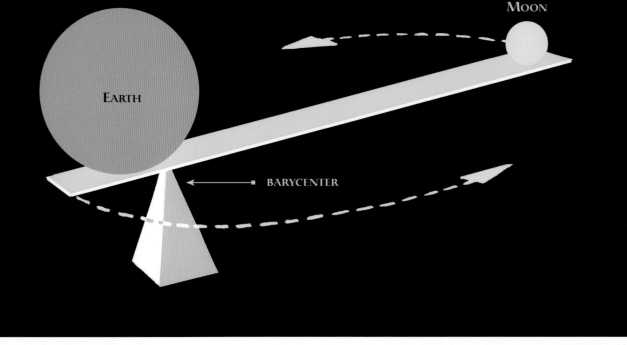

This diagram shows the barycenter, or point around which the Earth and the Moon rotate.

Imagine two unequal weights connected by a string and spinning. That is how Earth and its Moon move through space. Because the barycenter lies within Earth, astronomers don't consider the Moon to be a planet. But the Moon is slowly moving away from Earth at a rate of about 1.5 inches (3.8 centimeters) per year. As the Moon moves away, the barycenter moves closer to the surface of Earth. Eventually the barycenter will be above Earth's surface. When this happens many millions of years from now, Earth and its Moon will officially become a double planet.

RADAR TO THE *Moon*

On January 10, 1946, the U. S. Army Signal Corps sent a first radar signal to the Moon. It was the same kind of radar beam a traffic police officer uses to time a speeding car. A radar antenna sends out a small burst of electronic energy. When this beam strikes an object, it bounces back, like an echo. A second antenna detects this echo. The burst of radar energy sent to the Moon traveled at nearly the speed of light. A little more than two seconds after it was sent, scientists on Earth detected the echo.

> *"Beautiful! Beautiful! Magnificent desolation!"*
> —Edwin "Buzz" Aldrin, Apollo 11 *astronaut, as he stepped on the surface of the Moon for the first time, 1969*

SIGHTSEEING ON THE MOON

The Moon is only 240,000 miles (386,000 km) away from Earth. This is more than 150 times closer than the planet Mars is to Earth. Because the Moon is nearby and easy to reach, it will probably be the first stop for future space tourists. The Moon has many interesting places for tourists to visit.

Copernicus Crater is one of the Moon's most beautiful sights. It lies close to the center of the Moon as seen from Earth. At 58 miles (93 km) wide—about the same size as Yellowstone Park—it is easily visible through a pair of binoculars. The bright crater is surrounded by a white halo. The bright color probably comes from rock that was made into a fine powder during the explosion that created the crater. Since Copernicus sits by itself in one of the dark, flat areas of the Moon called *maria*, or "seas," it's very easy to spot. If you could stand on the crater's rim, you would be more than 0.5 mile (1 km) above the surrounding plain. In front you would see the slopes of the crater,

The Lunar Orbiter took this image of the Moon's Copernicus Crater in the 1960s.

> *"Copernicus is . . . the monarch [king] of the lunar ring-mountains."*
>
> —Thomas Gwyn Elger, British science writer, 1895

terraced like steps, leading to the floor nearly 2.5 miles (3.8 km) below. Unlike most other large craters on the Moon, Copernicus never filled with lava. Its floor is deep and bowl-like. Several peaks rise up in the center of the crater. Three of them reach 4,000 feet (1,200 km).

The South Pole-Aitken Basin is the largest crater on the Moon. It is also one of the largest known craters in the entire solar system. The crater is 1,392 miles (2,240 km) in diameter and 8 miles (13 km) deep. It is the result of a collision with an asteroid millions of years ago. (Asteroids are rocky bodies tens of feet to many miles across. Most of them orbit between Mars and Jupiter.) If the same crater were on Earth, it would stretch from New York City to Kansas City, Missouri.

This illustration shows how the South Pole-Aitken Basin would have been created millions of years ago when an asteroid collided with the Moon. Earth is in the bottom left corner.

CHECKING OUT THE MOON'S *Surface*

Russia (then part of the Soviet Union) was the first country to fly a space probe (exploring spacecraft) past the Moon. The *Luna 1* came within 3,100 miles (5,000 km) of the Moon in 1959. Over the next ten years, Russia and the United States launched more than fifty more probes. Only a handful reached their target. Russia's *Luna 2* was the first spacecraft to reach the lunar surface. Not meant to land, it crashed into the Moon like a speeding bullet. Another Russian spacecraft, *Luna 9*, made the first safe landing on the Moon in 1966. It took pictures and recorded information. The *Surveyor 1*, launched by the United States, also made a safe landing on the Moon in 1966. It took photos of the surface and tested samples of the soil. As it turned out, the lunar soil is firm, like wet beach sand. At the same time, the United States also launched several Lunar Orbiter spacecraft. These circled the Moon, taking thousands of photos. Not only was this information valuable for learning more about the Moon, it was also useful in finding a safe landing spot for future astronauts.

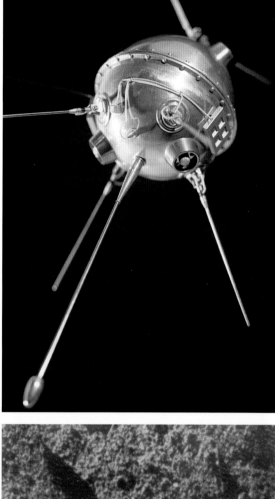

Top: *Russia's* Luna 2 *was the first spacecraft to reach the lunar surface in 1959.*
Bottom: *This photograph was taken by Russia's* Luna 9, *the first spacecraft to land on the Moon, in 1966.*

Mount Pico is a pyramid-shaped mountain rising 1.5 miles (2.4 km) above the surrounding lunar landscape. It is part of a ring of mountains that once completely surrounded a giant crater. Millions of years ago, lava flooded this crater and then hardened. This created a vast, flat, circular plain called the Mare Imbrium. (*Mare* means "sea" in Latin.) The lava buried most of the oldest mountains. Only a few peaks remain, like islands in a sea of stone. Mount Pico is the tallest of them.

The Straight Wall is an enormous cliff. It stands out by itself in another

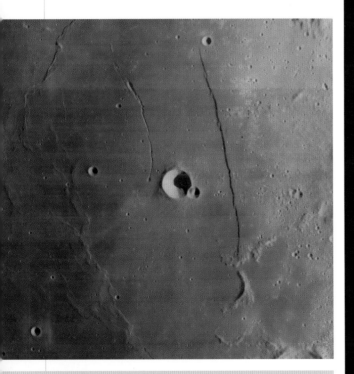

The Moon's Straight Wall is visible from Earth with a small telescope.

MEN ON THE *Moon*

On July 20, 1969, two astronauts safely landed on the surface of the Moon. This was the U.S. Apollo 11 mission. Astronauts Neil Armstrong and Buzz Aldrin *(below)* explored the area around their lander for two and a half hours. They were the first humans to walk on another world. Five more missions followed (a sixth had to turn back because of an accident). The last people to walk on the Moon were the astronauts who took part in the Apollo 17 mission in 1972. The Apollo program taught scientists much about what the Moon is made of and where it came from.

This illustration shows Mount Pico rising above the lunar surface.

flat, smooth plain. The wall is almost perfectly straight and nearly 75 miles (120 km) long. It was created when a huge block of the Moon's crust pushed upward along a fault, or a crack. Estimates of its height range from 820 to 1,300 feet (250 to 400 m). By comparison, the Great Wall of China is only 30 feet (9 m) high. The Straight Wall is easy to spot through a small telescope. It is a favorite subject for amateur astronomers.

The Moon is not only a wonder of the rocky planets. It is one of the special wonders of the entire solar system.

"For when I look at the Moon I do not see a hostile, empty world. I see the radiant body where man has taken his first steps into a frontier that will never end."

—*David R. Scott, commander,* Apollo 15, *1973*

MYSTERIOUS *Venus*

Venus looks like a cloudy pearl floating in space.

$\mathcal{V}$ENUS, NAMED FOR THE ROMAN GODDESS OF LOVE, LOOKS LIKE A GLEAMING WHITE PEARL FLOATING IN SPACE. ASTRONOMERS CALL VENUS EARTH'S SISTER PLANET. IT IS ALMOST EXACTLY THE SAME SIZE AS EARTH. VENUS'S ORBIT IS CLOSER TO EARTH THAN ANY OTHER PLANET IN OUR SOLAR SYSTEM. ITS ORBIT AROUND THE SUN CAN TAKE IT AS CLOSE TO EARTH AS 25 MILLION MILES (40 MILLION KM).

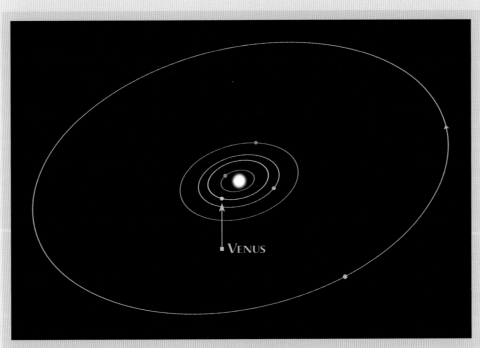

Venus orbits close to Earth, but it is nothing like Earth.

Venus is made of rock and metals as is Earth. It even has a dense atmosphere, or layer of gas, just as Earth does. Of all the worlds in the solar system, Venus should be most like our own. But its beauty and likeness to Earth don't prepare anyone for what the planet is really like. It is as though Venus wears a beautiful mask.

VENUS HIDDEN

For a long time, people knew very little about Venus. The planet is entirely covered in a thick layer of clouds. All anyone can see through a telescope from Earth is the top of this cloud cover. So Venus looks like a featureless, creamy ball. No one could even tell the length of a Venus day. With no surface features to use as landmarks, scientists could not measure its rotation. Guesses ranged from 22 hours to 224 days.

Not being able to see the surface of Venus did not stop astronomers from guessing about it. They knew that Venus was practically a twin of Earth in size. Many scientists thought that since Venus is closer to the Sun than Earth is, it would be warmer than Earth. The thick clouds might mean a humid atmosphere with constant rain. They pictured a jungle world, like Earth during the age of the dinosaurs. Other astronomers thought that Venus had no land at all. They thought it was covered by a worldwide ocean. Others argued that the planet was a dry, lifeless desert. They thought it had been eroded by powerful winds and baked by a temperature as high as that of boiling water.

Astronomers finally solved the question of Venus's rotation in the 1960s. Radar beamed from Earth penetrated Venus's clouds. The radar showed that Venus rotates backward! Earth and the other planets in the solar system rotate from west to east (counterclockwise as seen from above their north poles). Venus slowly spins from east to west, or clockwise. It takes Venus 243 days to make one rotation. Why Venus rotates this way is one more mystery about the planet.

Astronomers used radar and satellite data to create this image of the surface of Venus.

THE OVEN WORLD

Astronomers knew that Venus had a dense atmosphere. But what it was made of was a mystery for two centuries. In 1932 astronomers at the Mount Wilson Observatory in California detected huge amounts of carbon dioxide (CO_2) in the atmosphere of Venus. This is the same gas you exhale when you breathe. It also forms the bubbles in soda pop. Venus's atmosphere is 96 percent carbon dioxide.

In the 1960s, the surface temperature of Venus was figured to be about 891°F (477°C). This temperature is high enough to melt lead and tin. The high

"There are so many stars shining in the sky, so many beautiful things winking at you, but when Venus comes out, all the others are waned, they are pushed to the background."

—*Mehmet Murat Ildan, from his play* Galileo Galilei, *1970*

temperature showed that Venus was not a tropical world and didn't have huge oceans. Oceans would have boiled away at that temperature.

Russian scientists managed to land a probe on the surface of Venus in 1970. The probe confirmed the high temperature. The probe also measured an atmospheric pressure at the surface. It was ninety times that of Earth. The weight of Earth's atmosphere pressing down on the planet's surface is 14 pounds per square inch (1 kilogram per sq. cm). A visitor to Venus would have to withstand a pressure of 1,260 pounds on every square inch (89 kg per sq. cm) of his or her body. This is 90 tons per square foot (8.8 metric tons per sq. m). It is equal to the pressure under 3,000 feet (1,000 m) of water. Such pressure would crush most submarines. The main reason for this pressure is that CO_2 is much heavier than the oxygen and nitrogen that make up the atmosphere of Earth. Since CO_2 weighs so much more, it presses down more heavily on the surface of Venus.

ACID CLOUDS

Astronomers solved the mystery of Venus's clouds in the early 1970s. They found that the clouds are not made up of water droplets, like earthly clouds. Instead, they

ANOTHER VENUS *Mystery*

When Venus is between Earth and the Sun, the unlit side (facing away from the Sun) is still visible as a dim, gray disk. Astronomers call this glow "ashen light." They wonder what creates it. Sometimes, when Earth's Moon is just a thin crescent in the sky, its dark side can be seen as a faint gray circle. This image is caused by sunlight reflected from Earth onto the Moon. But Venus has no moons, so its own moonlight cannot be lighting it. In the nineteenth century, an astronomer suggested that the glow might be from vast forest fires burning on Venus. That would be impossible, since Venus has no life, let alone forests or the oxygen needed for fires to burn. Could some sort of chemical reaction in Venus's strange atmosphere be causing the glow? Could it have something to do with lightning? Could it be similar to the northern and southern lights that flicker around the North Pole and the South Pole on Earth? No one knows.

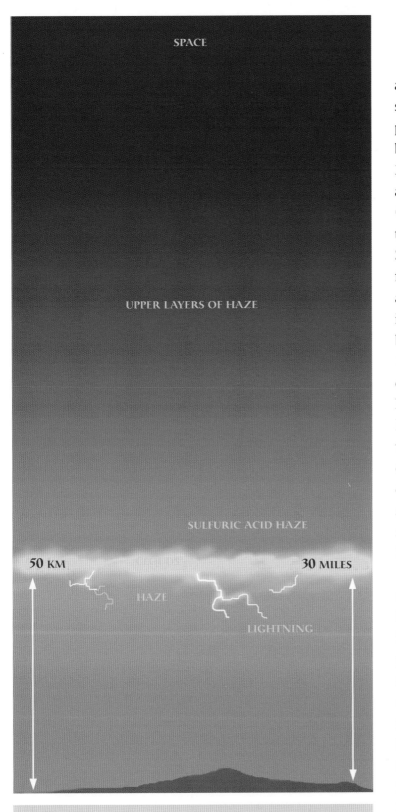

Within the illustration:

SPACE

UPPER LAYERS OF HAZE

SULFURIC ACID HAZE

50 KM   30 MILES

HAZE

LIGHTNING

This illustration shows the layers of the atmosphere of Venus.

are made of tiny droplets of sulfuric acid. This is the same powerful acid found in car batteries. These acid clouds are 30 to 36 miles (48 to 58 km) above the surface of Venus. (Clouds on Earth average less than 6 miles, or 10 km, high.) Sulfuric acid rain probably falls from these clouds. The acid rain evaporates (dries up) in the hot atmosphere long before it reaches the ground. In 1978 Russian and U.S. probes discovered powerful bolts of lightning within the clouds. But beneath this cloud layer, the atmosphere seems to be clear. Instead of the gloomy, dark world imagined by many science fiction writers, the surface of Venus is as bright as a lightly overcast day on Earth.

The planet Mercury is almost twice as close to the Sun as Venus is. Yet its surface is nowhere near as hot. On a planet that lacks an atmosphere, such as Mercury, the heat its surface receives from the Sun travels back out into space. But if the planet has an atmosphere, as Venus does, the atmosphere traps much of the incoming heat from the Sun.

This kind of heating is called a greenhouse effect. The glass panes of a greenhouse allow the Sun's light and heat to enter but prevent the heat inside from escaping. The heat builds up inside the greenhouse until it becomes hotter than outside. Venus's atmosphere is almost entirely CO_2 (carbon dioxide). CO_2 is a greenhouse gas. It traps the Sun's heat on Venus, causing the very high temperatures.

Since Venus resembles Earth in every other way, why is its atmosphere so different? One reason is Earth's oceans. CO_2 dissolves easily in water. Earth may once have had as much CO_2 as Venus, but its oceans absorbed most of it.

GLOBAL *Warming*

Two gases are particularly good at trapping heat from the Sun. These are water vapor and carbon dioxide. The two are called greenhouse gases. Fortunately for life on our world, Earth has just enough of these gases to keep it pleasantly warm, but not too hot for life to exist. If the amount of greenhouse gases increased, the average temperature of Earth would increase too. The average temperature of Earth has risen in the last century. This warming seems to be clearly linked to the use of fossil fuels, such as coal, natural gas, and petroleum. When burned, these fuels produce CO_2, which ends up in Earth's atmosphere.

The diagram shows how the greenhouse effect heats a planet.

Powerful infrared radiation from the Sun penetrates the atmosphere and heats the surface.

Infrared radiation from the surface is too weak to escape through the atmosphere back into space.

Since the surface receives more heat than can escape, it grows hotter and hotter.

Sapas Mons is a large volcano on the surface of Venus. This false-color image shows the lava flows that extend into the landscape.

CRATERS AND VOLCANOES

Most of Venus's volcanoes are small shield volcanoes. Shield volcanoes form when lava flows out evenly from the interior of the planet through a vent in its surface. On Venus the volcanoes gradually build up into a wide, low mound. Most are less than 13 miles (20 km) in diameter.

Some of Venus's larger shield volcanoes resemble enormous, flat pancakes. They measure 13 to 60 miles (20 to 100 km) wide. They were formed by very thick lava flowing slowly over the surface, like heavy pancake batter poured onto a skillet. The largest of Venus's volcanoes resemble the big volcanoes of Earth. Sapas Mons on Venus is a typical large shield volcano. It is nearly 5,000 feet (1,500 m) high. The lava that poured from it flowed for more than 200 miles (320 km) over the surrounding landscape.

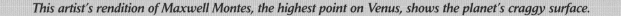

This artist's rendition of Maxwell Montes, the highest point on Venus, shows the planet's craggy surface.

Venus also has about one thousand giant meteorite craters, formed by collisions with rocks that have flown through space. Some of the craters are up to 124 miles (200 km) wide. Very few craters are smaller than 1.25 miles (2 km) wide. This lack of small craters is also a result of Venus's extraordinarily thick atmosphere. Small meteoroids (meteorites while they are still in space) break up long before they can reach the ground. Only the largest objects have enough energy to hit the surface.

Scientists were surprised at how well preserved Venus's craters are. The craters also seem to be scattered evenly over its entire surface. Earth, the Moon, and Mars all have ancient heavily cratered regions mixed with younger lightly cratered areas. In contrast, the surface of Venus seems to be about the same age everywhere. The surface also seems to be relatively young. Using the craters on the Moon as a guide, it would seem that Venus's surface isn't much older than about 500 million years. This might seem to be very old, but it is only about 10 percent of Venus's history. Why the surface of Venus appears to be so young is another great puzzle for scientists.

Astronomers have suggested that lava flowing from the volcanoes covers meteorite craters almost as fast as they form. This process would also explain why most of the craters seem young. Another idea is that about 500 million years ago, a vast volcanic eruption covered the entire planet with lava. The lava would have filled in all Venus's ancient craters. All the craters on Venus would have formed since then.

THE STRANGE CORONAS

The U.S. *Magellan* orbiter circling Venus discovered many other strange features. Among them are enormous target-shaped regions called coronas. Ranging from 130 to 1,300 miles (200 to 2,000 km) across, they were probably formed by molten rock lifting the surface from below. Because the surface of Venus is so hot, most of the rocks in its crust are only a few hundred degrees from melting temperature. Rocks as hot as this bend like taffy under pressure. In the past, molten rock underground might have formed giant bubbles. These bubbles might have sagged as the molten rock flowed out from beneath them. This sagging could have caused the rings of circular ridges and the cracks of the coronas.

Venus is a wonder for many reasons. There is no other world like it in all the solar system. With its rugged landscape, acid rains, crushing pressure, and furnace heat, it may never be visited by tourists. Future sightseers may gaze on it in awe—but from a distance.

This illustration shows Mars as seen from the larger of its moons—Phobos.

$\mathcal{I}$MAGINE A WORLD WHERE—INSTEAD OF CLOUDS—MOUNTAINS, CANYONS, AND PLAINS SLOWLY DRIFT OVERHEAD. IT WOULD BE LIKE THE VIEW FROM AN AIRPLANE, EXCEPT YOU WOULD BE LOOKING UP INSTEAD OF DOWN. THIS WOULD BE THE VIEW FROM PHOBOS, ONE OF THE TWO TINY MOONS OF MARS.

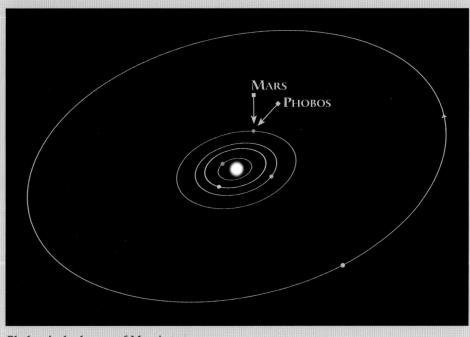

Phobos is the larger of Mars's two moons.

Up until the middle of the 1800s, many astronomers searched for moons around the Red Planet. None was successful. But Asaph Hall, a professor of mathematics at the U.S. Naval Observatory in Washington, D.C., was tired of reading that Mars had no moons. In 1877 he decided to look for himself.

He searched through a telescope for weeks with no luck and decided to give up. His wife insisted that he keep trying. Mars, she argued, would not be so close to Earth again for many years. It would be a long time before anyone had a chance to search for moons again. So Hall went back to his telescope.

On the nights of August 15, 16, 20, and 21, 1877, Hall found two tiny pinpoints of light, nearly lost in the glare of the planet itself. He had discovered Mars's moons. He called them Phobos and Deimos—"Fear" and "Terror." These were the names of the warhorses of Mars, the Roman god of war.

No one knew what these moons looked like. They were far too tiny to be visible as more than specks of light. It wasn't until 1969 that a spacecraft beamed the first photos of the moons back to Earth. These photos revealed a pair of dark, cratered, potato-shaped rocks.

The larger moon, Phobos, has a very large crater named Stickney, the maiden name of Hall's wife. It was named in her honor for encouraging Hall to continue his search. Stickney is 5 miles (8 km) wide. If the object that created Stickney had been any larger, the impact would have broken Phobos into pieces.

Top: *Asaph Hall was the first person to identify Mars's moons.*
Bottom: *The Stickney crater at left on Phobos is named after Hall's wife, Angeline Stickney.*

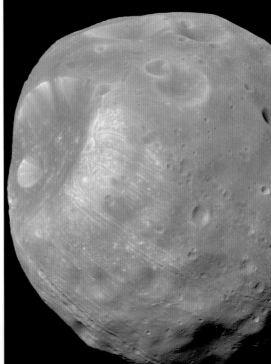

Many unusual grooves stretch around the little moon. Some of them are as wide as 300 feet (100 m) and as long as 6 miles (10 km). They seem to radiate away from Stickney. They may be cracks caused by the impact of the meteorite that created the crater.

Except for the similarity in color, Deimos, the smaller moon, looks very different from Phobos. It is much smoother, with far fewer craters. Many boulders lie on its surface. Its gravity, or pull, is very weak. If you were to drop a rock from eye level on Deimos, it would take nearly thirty seconds to hit the ground. This is fifty times longer than a rock dropped on Earth.

These two pictures show the relative sizes of Mars's moons—Deimos (left) and Phobos.

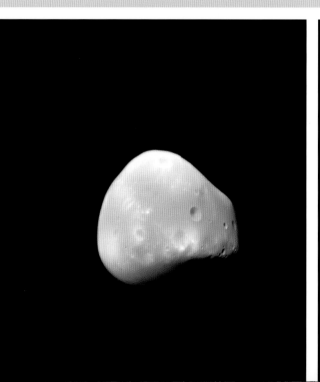
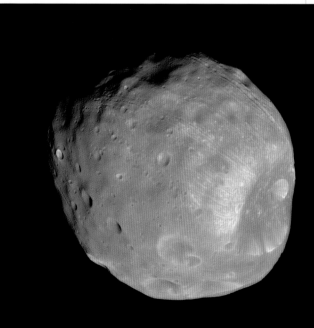

THE MOONS OF *Mars*

Name	Date of Discovery	Distance from Mars* miles (km)	Size** miles (km)
Phobos	1877	5,827 (9,377)	17 × 12 (27 × 19)
Deimos	1877	14,579 (23,463)	10 × 6 (16 × 10)

*As measured from the center of Mars

**Mars's moons are not spherical. They are shaped a little like potatoes. In this case, the longest and narrowest dimensions are given.

Seen from Mars, neither moon seems very interesting. Because they are so small, even the nearest one, Phobos, would look like a large, bright star. Deimos would just be a bright point of light in the Martian sky. What sets them apart from the other objects in the night sky is their speed. Phobos circles Mars in only 7.7 Earth hours. A day on Mars is about 24 hours. This means that Phobos circles Mars faster than Mars itself rotates. Once Phobos has risen, it takes only 4.4 hours to zoom through the sky and set again. Deimos, on the other hand, orbits Mars in 30.3 hours. This is about 6 hours longer than a Martian day. Deimos creeps very slowly across the night sky. More than 60 hours pass between Deimos-rise and Deimos-set.

A GIANT BEACH BALL

The view of Mars from its moons would be far more wondrous than the view of the moons seen from the planet. From Deimos, Mars would resemble a huge reddish orange beach ball. It would look more than thirty times bigger than the Moon looks from Earth. But the view from Phobos would be even more spectacular. Mars would fill Phobos's whole sky, looming more than eighty times larger than a full Earth Moon. Phobos always keeps one face toward Mars. This means that Mars is always hanging overhead on that side. It would look like a huge, circular, orange ceiling. The Martian landscape would always be changing as Phobos circled Mars in its orbit.

Many scientists believe that Phobos is doomed. It is so close to Mars's thin outer atmosphere that it is slowing down. Even at the distance Phobos is from

Mars, there is still a little bit of air. The moon has to move through it, like a boat sailing through water. If you give a toy boat a shove, it will move a few feet and then the water will slow it to a stop. Just as the water slowed the boat down, the particles of air are gradually slowing Phobos. In a few million years, its orbit will have slowed so much that Phobos will crash into Mars.

This illustration of the Mars surface shows Phobos in the sky (upper left).

MYSTERY MOONS

Scientists wonder about the origin of the two little moons. Were they formed in orbit around Mars the way Earth's Moon was? Are they the remnants of a larger moon that was broken up by a massive impact? One possible clue to their origin is that they are both very dark. Both moons look very much like the close-up photos of asteroids that have been taken by visiting spacecraft. It may be that Phobos and Deimos are asteroids that were captured by Mars's gravity.

As objects themselves, there is nothing very special about Phobos and Deimos. What makes them special is where they are. Orbiting so close to Mars, they have a view unlike anything else in the solar system.

Jonathan Swift wrote about the moons of Mars in the early 1700s, more than 150 years before they were discovered.

A STRANGE MYSTERY ABOUT THE MOONS *of Mars*

In his famous novel *Gulliver's Travels* (1726), Jonathan Swift wrote: "They [the Laputians] have likewise discovered two lesser Stars, or *Satellites*, which revolve about *Mars*, . . . the former revolves in the space of ten Hours, and the latter in Twenty-one and a Half . . . which evidently shows them to be governed by the same Law of Gravitation, that influences the other heavenly Bodies."

This is an almost perfect description of the orbits of Phobos and Deimos. What makes it remarkable is that it was written by 1726, a century and a half before Asaph Hall discovered them! How did Swift know there were two moons? How did he know that the innermost moon circled Mars in less than one Martian day? This knowledge is especially strange since this behavior is unique in the solar system. No other moon circles its planet faster than its planet rotates. Was his description just a coincidence, or did Swift have some special knowledge?

Seen from Mars's tiny moon, Phobos, the planet looks gigantic. Here we see the distant Sun setting behind Mars as Phobos moves into the planet's shadow.

6 Mercury

Mercury is the smallest planet as well as the closest planet to the Sun.

$\mathscr{M}$ERCURY, THE PLANET CLOSEST TO THE SUN, IS A BATTERED LITTLE WORLD. ITS SKY IS FILLED WITH THE SUN NEARLY THREE TIMES LARGER THAN IT APPEARS FROM EARTH. NINE TIMES MORE LIGHT AND HEAT POUR DOWN ONTO MERCURY THAN ONTO EARTH. THE CRAGGY SURFACE CAN REACH A TEMPERATURE OF 800°F (427°C). THIS IS HOT ENOUGH TO MELT LEAD, TIN, AND ZINC.

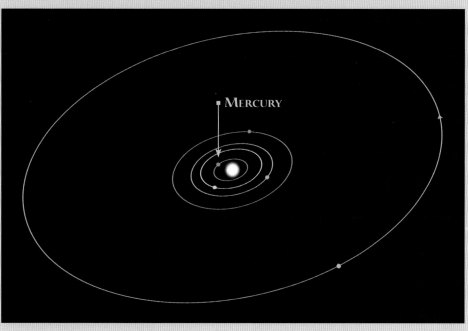

Mercury orbits closest to the Sun.

The Sun rises over the horizon of Mercury in this illustration.

Mercury is so close to the Sun that it must have formed from elements and minerals that could survive such high temperatures. These include metals with high melting points and silicates, rocks that contain the element silicon. Water and minerals with low melting points were all burned up by the Sun and blown away. Its concentration of metal makes Mercury unusually heavy for such a small world.

Mercury has been battered by asteroids and other space debris since its formation. Most places on its surface bear the scars of thousands of craters. The planet appears to be a dead world. Other than impacts, nothing seems to have happened on the planet for the last 3 or 4 billion years.

Mercury's Weird Days

The gravity of the close-by Sun has slowed Mercury's rotation. It takes the planet fifty-nine days to rotate on its axis. Mercury's orbit around the Sun takes eighty-eight days.

The craters on Mercury's surface record a violent history.

The combination of a slow rotation and short year means that the Sun seems to move very slowly through Mercury's sky. It takes 176 Earth days between one sunrise and the next. The Sun appears to stop, move backward for a while, and then stop again before it continues on across Mercury's sky. At some places on Mercury, you would be able to see two sunrises and two sunsets every Mercury day.

Because Mercury's days are so long, the surface of the planet gets very hot. Afternoon temperatures can reach 441°F (227°C). Nights are just as long and can be extremely cold, with temperatures dropping to −279°F (−173°C). Unlike the Earth or Venus, Mercury has no atmosphere to hold in heat. Whatever warmth it receives from the Sun during the day quickly travels back out into space at night. Even though Mercury is closer to the Sun than Venus is, it doesn't get as hot.

FACTS ABOUT *Mercury*

Diameter: 3,031 miles (4,878 km)

Average Distance from the Sun: 36 million miles (58 million km)

Length of Year: 88 Earth days

Length of Day: 59 Earth days

MERCURY'S GIANT CRATER

A visitor to Mercury would see thousands of craters. They come in every size, from the tiniest potholes to giants hundreds of miles across. The Caloris Basin, the biggest of these craters, is 807 miles (1,300 km) wide. It is one of the largest impact craters in the entire solar system. The basin was created millions of years ago when a large asteroid slammed into Mercury. From space, Caloris Basin looks like a series of circles, like frozen ripples. The Caloris Montes, or "Mountains," form the outermost ring. They are almost 1.25 miles (2 km) high.

The impact that created Caloris Basin may have done more than just make a huge crater. On the side of Mercury opposite the center of Caloris is a region of rugged hills. These may have formed when pressure waves from the asteroid impact traveled around Mercury. These are the same sorts of waves as the waves that form when you throw a stone into a pool of water. When the waves met on the other side, they would have torn up the landscape. The hills might have been the result.

MERCURY'S EVENING AND *Morning Stars*

From Earth, Venus is often visible as a very bright star in the early morning or early evening. If you were to visit Mercury, you would see Venus as a bright star in Mercury's sky too. It would be even brighter than it appears from Earth. You would often see a second star, almost as bright as Venus shining with a blue light. It would be planet Earth. Earth shines bright enough to cast faint shadows on the dark ground of Mercury *(artist's illustration below)*. If your eyes were very sharp, you might even spot a tiny pinpoint of light next to Earth—the Moon.

"A summer vacation on Mercury
would not be much fun."
—Roy A. Gallant, author, 1980

The inside of the Caloris Basin contains radiating cracks, or troughs, that have been nicknamed the Spider.
Scientists think they were created when the floor of the basin cracked apart.

Amazing Cliffs

Slicing across Mercury's surface are several long cliffs. They stretch for up to 311 miles (500 km). Some are nearly 2.5 miles (4 km) high, more than twice as high as the walls of the Grand Canyon. These cliffs cut through mountains, craters, and valleys like cracks in broken glass. They were created when Mercury's surface cracked just like glass. This happened as Mercury cooled after its formation. As it cooled, it shrank. This shrinking caused the crust on its surface to settle and crack. On one side of some cracks, the land pushed up. On the other side, it fell. Cliffs that are created this way are called scarps.

This artwork shows the rocky surface of Mercury.

The large cliffs on Mercury were created by the shrinking of the surface as the planet cooled after its formation.

Mercury has scarps that have split huge craters in half. One half of one crater is raised nearly 10,000 feet (3,000 m) above the other half.

Mercury is a strange little world. It is wonderful not so much for what it is but for where it is. Future space tourists may make brief stops on its rugged, scorched surface. There they will watch in amazement as a giant Sun rises above the horizon to perform weird acrobatics unlike anything seen in the skies of Earth.

"I had rather be Mercury, the smallest among seven [planets], revolving round the sun, than the first among five [moons] revolving round Saturn."

—Johann Wolfgang von Goethe, German author, 1772

7 Life ON EARTH

Earth as viewed from space shows oceans, continents, and clouds swirling in the atmosphere.

THE FINAL WONDER OF THE SOLAR SYSTEM IS READING THIS SENTENCE. OTHER PLANETS HAVE GREAT CANYONS, TOWERING MOUNTAINS, AND GIANT VOLCANOES. BUT AS FAR AS ANYONE KNOWS, ONLY EARTH HAS LIFE. THE PRESENCE OF LIFE MAKES EARTH SPECIAL. ASTRONOMER CARL SAGAN THOUGHT THERE WERE NO OTHER WONDERS IN THE SOLAR SYSTEM. "FROM WHAT WE CURRENTLY KNOW ABOUT THE SOLAR SYSTEM," HE SAID, "I WOULD SAY THAT ALL SEVEN WONDERS SHOULD BE DRAWN FROM THE BIOLOGY OF EARTH."

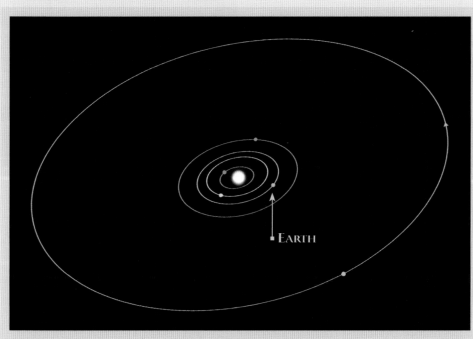

Earth's place in its solar orbit helped make it suitable for life.

Why Earth? At first glance, it might seem to be a perfectly average place. But one important feature sets it apart from all the other planets. The word *earth* simply means "dirt" or "land." But the first thing an alien visitor would notice is that the planet is blue. That's because Earth is mostly covered by water. Dry land makes up only about one-quarter of its surface. Our planet would have been much better named Ocean. No other planet in the solar system has open bodies of liquid water. Without liquid water, life may never have evolved on Earth.

A LIVING PLANET

Earth has almost two million different species, or kinds, of life. Scientists discover new species all the time. Life ranges from the algae growing on the side of a goldfish bowl to human beings. It can be a boneless jellyfish the size of your little fingernail or a giant blue whale. At up to 110 feet (33 m) long and 190 tons (172 metric tons), the giant blue whale is the largest animal that ever lived on Earth.

Life can be found from the frozen poles to the steaming equator. It is at the bottom of the ocean and miles in the air. It is in your backyard garden and in boiling hot springs. Yet all life on Earth shares a common thread. Every one of the plants and animals—including you—evolved from simple, one-celled organisms that came into being 3.8 billion years ago. As different as you may seem from your pet cat, a daffodil, or a jellyfish, the basic blueprints of all life go back to its very beginnings on this planet.

THE MAGIC *Liquid*

Water can dissolve more substances than any other liquid, including the most powerful acids. When water passes through rock or soil, it dissolves and carries away chemicals, minerals, and nutrients important for life. The oceans are salty because they are filled with minerals and nutrients water has carried from the land. If water had not been able to do this, the seas would be empty of life.

Water is vital for all living things. Nearly 60 percent of your body is water. About 83 percent of your blood is water. The water makes it possible for your blood to dissolve many different kinds of materials because of the water in it. Blood can carry nutrients to every cell, transport their wastes, and control the temperature of your body.

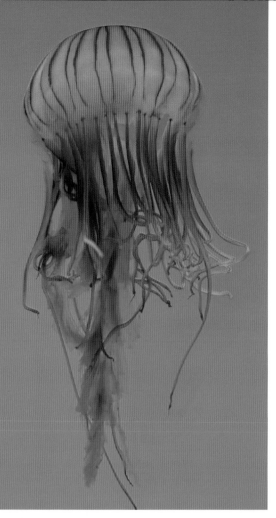

Jellyfish (left), daffodils (above), and blue whales (below) are examples of the variety of life on Earth.

Where Life Came From

Between 4.2 and 3.5 billion years ago, vast oceans covered Earth. These oceans were a soup of minerals and elements eroded from the land by wind, rain, and meteor impacts. The water also had large amounts of carbon dioxide dissolved in it. The chemical-filled oceans, combined with the energy provided by sunlight, lightning, and tides, were the ingredients required for the beginning of life.

Billions of molecules (combinations of two or more atoms, the smallest bits of all things) formed in this rich chemical soup. Some of these molecules were able to reproduce themselves. They developed into more complex life-forms. No one knows exactly when the first true living cells evolved from these early, reproducing molecules. We do know that by at least 3.5 billion years ago, Earth contained true living cells. Scientists have found their remains in some of the oldest rocks on our planet.

The first simple life-forms to inhabit Earth were bacteria and their relatives, the blue-green algae. Both are still with us, making them the oldest and most successful life-forms on our planet.

Blue-green algae grows in a lake. Blue-green algae is a simple life-form that is one of the oldest on Earth.

Bacteria World

The most abundant life-form on Earth is also the smallest. Bacteria are tiny, one-celled organisms. Most are only a few micrometers in length (1 micrometer equals 0.00004 inches). Most bacteria are harmless. Some are useful, such as those that make cheese or decompose waste products. Others are vital to human life. The ones that live in human intestines help digest food. Some bacteria are dangerous. Cholera and anthrax are diseases caused by bacteria. The plague, which killed millions of people in Europe in the fourteenth century, was caused by bacteria.

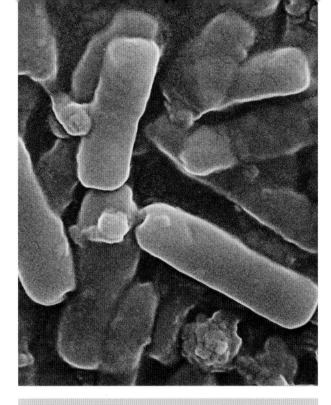

Above: *Bacteria are the most abundant life-forms on Earth and can be found nearly everywhere.*
Below: *This illustration shows the structure of DNA (deoxyribonucleic acid), the blueprint of life.*

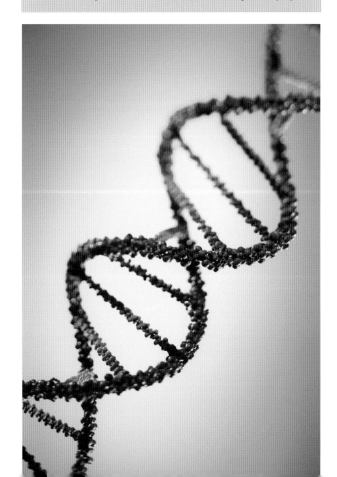

Pound for pound, there are more bacteria on this planet than any other kind of life. Every 0.03 ounces (1 gram) of soil contains about 40 million bacteria. This totals about five nonillion (5,000,000,000,000,000,000,000,000,000,000) bacteria on Earth. If you could put them all on a scale, they would far outweigh all the plants and the animals on Earth combined. Even you are mostly bacteria. There are more bacteria living in your digestive system and on your skin than there are cells in your body.

THE ARRIVAL OF DNA

Between 2 and 3 billion years ago, a brand-new type of cell came into being. Unlike the cells of bacteria or blue-green algae, these new cells had a nucleus. This is a tiny clump in their middle like the pit of a peach. The nucleus was protected by a membrane, a thin covering. The new cell's DNA (deoxyribonucleic acid) was gathered in the nucleus. DNA is a giant molecule that contains an animal's or a plant's blueprint. It is the set of instructions a cell needs to create copies of itself. Concentrating DNA into one place in a cell made it easier for a cell to reproduce. Two types of these improved cells eventually evolved. One type resembled the original algae and was the ancestor of plants. The other version, called protozoa, evolved into animals.

THE LIVING LAND: THE FORESTS

A visitor from another planet seeing our world for the first time would probably be amazed at how green Earth is. None of the other rocky planets are green. Earth is green because 30 percent of the dry land of Earth is covered by forests. One important kind of forest on Earth is the rain forest. At least 68 to 78 inches (175 to 200 cm) of rain falls on rain forests every year. Every continent except Antarctica has them. Most of the world's rain forests are tropical rain forests. They are found near the equator. Another kind of rain forest is the temperate rain forest. These lie in cooler regions. The great forests of the northwestern United States are the largest temperate rain forests on Earth.

Rain forests are sometimes called "the lungs of the world." Plants release oxygen into the air as they grow. Rain forests produce 28 percent of the world's oxygen. More than 20 percent of that total is produced by the rain forest around the Amazon River in South America. In addition, one-fifth of the world's freshwater lies in the Amazon River basin.

The tropical rain forests are rich in life. More than half of the world's estimated 10 million species of plants, animals, and insects live there. An area of just 4 square miles (10 sq. km) may contain as many as fifteen hundred different flowering plants, 750 species of trees, and four hundred species of birds.

Rain forests, such as this one in Puerto Rico, contain and help support an amazing variety of life.

Coral reefs, such as this one in Indonesia, showcase the vast array of life in the ocean.

THE LIVING OCEANS

More than 2 million million tons (1.8 million million metric tons) of living things can be found on Earth. Of this great mass of life, 85 percent lives in the oceans that cover most of our planet. One of the smallest of these living things is one of the most important food sources. Tiny animals called plankton are eaten by fish and shellfish. The small fish and shellfish in turn are eaten by larger fish, birds, and sea mammals. Many of these larger animals are eaten by humans.

Tiny plants called algae are equally important. Between 70 and 80 percent of all the oxygen in the atmosphere is produced by algae. (Most living things need oxygen to breathe.) This comes to more than 330 billion tons (300 billion metric tons) of oxygen every year. Algae can take the form of individual, almost microscopic cells floating freely in the water. The green scum that grows on the surface of ponds and on the inside glass of aquariums is algae. Algae can also form giant colonies. Ordinary seaweed is nothing more than a colony of algae cells. Some kinds of seaweed are among the largest plants on Earth. One kind of seaweed, kelp, can grow to be 100 to 260 feet (30 to 80 m) long.

Even the inhospitable Sahara in Africa contains some life.

THE EXTREMOPHILES

Not every place on Earth would seem to be friendly to life. Permanently frozen ice caps are thousands of feet thick. At the bottom of the deep ocean are trenches, where sunlight never reaches and water pressure is measured in tons. Water boils from hot springs. Lakes are full of acid, and seas can be nearly nine times saltier than the ocean. In sun-baked desert regions, temperatures can reach 130°F (54°C). Less than 0.04 inches (1 millimeter) of rain may fall every year.

Yet life can be found in such hostile places. These life-forms are called extremophiles. The name comes from Latin words that mean "love of the extreme." Most extremophiles are tiny organisms. Many are bacteria. One type of bacteria lives by eating sulfur and turning it into sulfuric acid. Another type lives on oxygen in the air. It combines this with hydrogen, producing water as a waste product. Yet another bacteria gets its energy by using oxygen to turn iron into rust.

One kind of bacteria lives in solutions of up to 3 percent sulfuric acid, strong enough to burn skin. Other bacteria live in very salty places such as the Great Salt Lake in Utah and ponds in Antarctica that are as much as one-third salt. Bacteria that live at the bottom of deep ocean trenches resist pressures of more than 144,000 pounds per square inch (10,000 kg per sq. cm). Bacteria also have been found living in ice at depths of nearly 2 miles (3.2 km). Some can survive the temperatures of more than 300°F (150°C) around undersea volcanoes. Some live in the scalding water of hot springs, where temperatures may reach 177°F (80°C). The bright colors of many of the hot springs in Yellowstone National Park are the result of bacteria and algae.

Volcanic vents on the seafloor look like chimneys up to 10 feet (3 m) tall. Hot water mixed with minerals erupts from them. The water can be as hot as 752°F (400°C). In spite of this heat, certain species of crabs, clams, and worms thrive near these vents.

The amazing colors in this hot spring at Yellowstone National Park are created by the presence of algae in the water.

Even hydrothermal vents on the ocean floor have creatures living near or in them.

The deepest part of Earth's oceans is almost 7 miles (11 km) beneath the surface. At that depth, the pressure of the water is immense. Sunlight cannot penetrate more than about 300 feet (100 m) below the surface. Everything is as dark as midnight. Yet fish and other creatures survive at these depths.

LIFE ELSEWHERE

Earth is the only planet known to have life. But this doesn't mean life can't exist on other worlds. The study of extremophiles shows us that life can show up in very hostile conditions. Perhaps other planets in the solar system have them.

Mars is one planet that might have living organisms. Many scientists are certain that signs of life will eventually be discovered there. Some hope to find

THE MARTIAN *Meteor*

Billions of years ago, an asteroid hit Mars. It created a huge explosion. A great many rocks from the surface of Mars flew off into space. Some of these rocks eventually reached Earth. In 1984 scientists found one of the Martian rocks. When they broke it open and peered inside through a microscope, they were astonished to discover what looked like fossil bacteria. Some scientists called this finding evidence that life evolved on Mars many millions of years ago. Others said they were a natural feature of the asteroid and had nothing to do with life. Recently, scientists discovered a kind of mineral surrounding the possible fossils that only living creatures can produce. Since astronomers know that Mars was once much warmer and wetter than it is today, this discovery may be proof that life once existed on Mars. The big question is: does any Martian life still exist?

some living things. Others would be happy if only fossils of extinct (died out) life-forms were found.

Millions of years ago, Mars was a wet world. It had seas and rivers, just as Earth does. It would have been easy for life to have evolved then. Since then, Mars has become a cold, dry planet. Temperatures can drop as low as −200°F (−130°C) at the poles in winter. At noon during a summer day, it can be as warm as 80°F (27°C). Scientists have recently learned that Mars still has plenty of water. It is all frozen and mostly underground. If life did exist on Mars in its watery past, it may have evolved to survive the changing environment. Earth's extremophiles show that it can be done.

INTELLIGENT LIFE

Many scientists believe that life begins easily, given the right conditions. So there may be many worlds—some even in our own solar system—on which life has evolved. But so far as we know, Earth is the only planet in the solar system on which intelligent life exists.

*"Earth is the cradle of humanity,
but one cannot live in the cradle forever."*
—Konstantin Tsiolkovsky, Russian spaceflight pioneer, 1899

For a very long time, humans liked to think that they were the only truly intelligent beings on Earth. But we've learned that there are many different kinds of intelligence. And there are also degrees of intelligence. Some of the basic standards for intelligence might include things like:

• The ability to adapt to new environments or changes in the environment
• A capacity for learning
• The ability to reason
• The ability to understand the connections between thoughts and things
• The ability to invent and form new ideas
• Self-awareness

Crowds of people make their way through Hong Kong, China, in 2009. Humans are one of the teeming life-forms that inhabit Earth.

ALIENS Listening In?

Long before any alien visitors reach Earth, they likely would have been able to tune into radio and television signals that have traveled many millions of miles into space. The signals from the first radio broadcasts are already more than 100 light-years away. A light-year is the distance light travels in one year. Light travels at 186,000 miles (300,000 km) per second, so the radio signals are 6 trillion miles (9.5 trillion km) from Earth. The star nearest Earth is only 4.5 light-years away.

Many of our spacecraft have already left the solar system. *Pioneer 10*, launched in 1972, is racing on nearly 7.6 billion miles (12 billion km) from Earth. *Pioneer 10* is traveling in the direction of the star Aldebaran, about 68 light-years away. *Pioneer 10* should arrive in about 2 million years.

What if intelligent beings live on a planet orbiting Aldebaran? What if they find our spacecraft? Just in case this happens, *Pioneer 10* carries a plaque with information about the creatures living on a distant planet called Earth. The plaque has a picture of a man and a woman. It also gives the location of our planet. It is like a message in a bottle, saying "Hello! We are here!" to some strange beings 2 million years in our future.

Most animals can do at least one or two of these things to some degree. Birds and chimpanzees can invent and use tools, dolphins use language, elephants live in complex societies, ants and beavers are excellent engineers, dogs and crows can reason, and parrots can do simple arithmetic. But humans have more of these abilities and can do many of them better than any other creatures on Earth.

An alien visitor coming to our solar system for the first time would find many wonderful things. They include giant mountains, huge volcanoes, and great canyons. But the thing an alien might find most wonderful is that the little blue planet is teeming with life.

TIMELINE

1877 U.S. astronomer Asaph Hall discovers the moons of Mars.

1946 The U.S. Army bounces a radar signal from the Moon.

1959 The Russian spacecraft *Luna 1* flies past the Moon.

1966 The Russian spacecraft *Luna 9* is the first to land on the Moon.

The U.S. spacecraft *Surveyor 1* also lands on the Moon.

1967 *Mariner 5* flies past Venus at a distance of less than 2,500 miles (4,000 km).

1969 U.S. astronauts walk on the moon.

1971 *Mariner 9* becomes the first spacecraft to orbit Mars. It takes the first close-up photos of the Martian moons.

1972 *Pioneer 10* is launched on a mission to Jupiter and Saturn.

1974 *Mariner 10* makes the first flyby of Mercury.

1990 *Magellan* goes into orbit around Venus. Its radar makes the first detailed maps of the surface.

1997 *Pathfinder* is the first rover to land on the surface of Mars.

2004 The *Messenger* spacecraft is launched on a mission to Mercury. It is scheduled to arrive in 2011 when it will become the first spacecraft to orbit the planet. The *Opportunity* and *Spirit* rovers land on Mars. They find evidence that water once existed on the surface.

2008 The *Phoenix* lander sets down in the north polar region of Mars. It discovers water ice just beneath the surface.

2010 Astronomers discover that a sunlike star HD 10180 has at least five planets, including a rocky planet almost the same size as Earth. Scientists find small fossil sponges in Australia that may be 640 to 650 million years old, 100 million years older than any previously known life-form.

CHOOSE AN EIGHTH WONDER

The solar system is filled with wonderful, amazing places. Do some research on your own or with a friend. See if you can discover some candidates for the Eighth Wonder of the Rocky Planets and their Moon.

To start your research, look through some of the books in the reading list or visit some of the websites. You will find hundreds of wonderful photos of amazing places on these planets. Look for wonders that
- *Have been recently discovered*
- *Show evidence of life beyond Earth*
- *Are extremely large or extremely small*

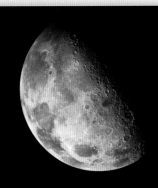

You might even try gathering photos and writing your own chapter on the eighth wonder. Scientists are making amazing new discoveries on the rocky planets and their moons all the time. Maybe you will be the scientist who finds the most amazing wonder of all.

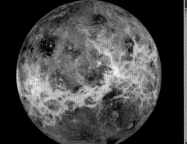

GLOSSARY

asteroid: one of the numerous small bodies composed of rock and metal that orbit (circle) the Sun, mainly between the orbits of Mars and Jupiter

astronomer: a scientist who studies stars and planets

atmosphere: the layer of gas that surrounds a moon or a planet

bacteria: tiny, single-celled organisms

barycenter: the point around which two bodies orbit

caldera: a large crater formed by the explosion of a volcano or by the collapse of its cone

crust: the outer surface of a planet or a moon

DNA: deoxyribonucleic acid; a complex molecule that carries genetic information

erosion: the wearing away of a landscape by wind, water, and other forces

extremophile: a plant or an animal that can survive in extreme conditions, such as great heat or cold

gravity: the force of attraction between two bodies, such as a planet and a moon

greenhouse effect: the warming of the surface of a planet by heat from the Sun trapped beneath the atmosphere

lava: molten rock flowing or that has flowed from a volcano

light-year: the distance light travels in one year. Light travels at a speed of 186,000 miles (300,000 km) per second, so a light-year is more than 6 trillion miles (10 trillion km).

meteorite: a stone or a rock that has fallen from space onto Earth

orbit: the circular or elliptical path taken by a moon as it circles a planet or a planet as it circles the Sun

radar: radio energy sent in a beam toward an object to determine the object's presence, size, and movement

rift valley: a long, winding, flat-floored valley formed when a planet's crust pulls apart along a crack

rille: a narrow, winding valley

scarp: a cliff formed when a block of a planet's crust splits along a crack and one part moves up while the other moves down

shield volcano: a volcano with shallow, sloping sides created by layers of lava flowing over a broad area

silicate: a compound that contains silicon, oxygen, and one or more metals. Much of Earth's crust is made of silicates.

space probe: an unmanned spacecraft sent to explore a planet or a moon

Source Notes

12 William K. Hartmann, *A Traveler's Guide to Mars* (New York: Workman Publishing, 2003), 349.

14 Edward Bernard, quoted in Gerard P. Kuiper, "On the Martian Surface Features," *Publications of the Astronomical Society of the Pacific* 67, no. 398 (October 1955): 271.

20 William K. Hartmann, *The New Mars* (Washington, DC: NASA, 1974), 87.

23 J. T. Maston, correspondence with author, May 8, 2009.

29 Edwin "Buzz' Aldrin, quoted in "NASA Honors Buzz Aldrin with Explorations Award," NASA, March 27, 2006, http://www.nasa.gov/vision/space/features/aldrin_ambassador_of_exploration.html (February 2, 2010).

30 Thomas Gwyn Elger, quoted in "Copernicus," Wikispaces, 2010, http://the-moon.wikispaces.com/Copernicus (May 6, 2010).

33 David R. Scott, "What Is It Like to Walk on the Moon?," *National Geographic* 144, no. 3 (September 1973), available online at "Eyes Turned Skyward," SpaceQuotations.com, 2010, http://www.spacequotations.com/moonquotes.html (May 6, 2010).

37 Mehmet Muran Ildan, in *Galileo Galilei*, available online at "Venus Quotes," Today in Science History, 2009, http://www.todayinsci.com/QuotationsCategories/V_Cat/Venus-Quotations.htm (May 6, 2010).

43 Carl Sagan, *Cosmos* (New York: Random House, 1980), 97.

47 Asaph Hall, quoted in Hartmann, *New Mars*, 149.

50 Jonathan Swift, quoted in Lee Krystek, "The Mysterious Moons of Mars," unmuseum .org, 1997, http://www.unmuseum.org/marsmoon.htm (February 14, 2010).

57 Roy A Gallant, *Our Universe* (Washington, DC: National Geographic, 1980), 69.

59 Johann Wolfgang von Goethe, in James Wood, *Dictionary of Quotations from Ancient and Modern, English and Foreign Sources* 166 (1893): 23, available online at "Saturn Quotes," Today in Science History, 2009, http://www.todayinsci.com/QuotationsCategories/S_Cat/Saturn-Quotations.htm (May 6, 2010).

61 Carl Sagan, correspondence with author, May 8, 1990.

71 Anaxagoras, quoted in "Quotations on Science and the Mysteries of the Universe," National Institute of Environmental Health Sciences, 2010, http://kids.niehs.nih.gov/quotes/qtscience.htm (February 2, 2010).

72 Ron Miller and William K. Hartmann, *The Grand Tour* (New York: Workman Publishing, 1984), 7.

Selected Bibliography

Beatty, J. Kelly, Carolyn Collins Petersen, and Andrew Chaikin, eds. *The New Solar System.* Cambridge, MA: Sky Publishing Corp., 1999.

Faure, Gunter, and Teresa Mensing. *Introduction to Planetary Science.* Dordrecht, Netherlands: Springer, 2007.

Hartmann, William K. *Moons and Planets.* Belmont, CA: Wadsworth Publishing Co., 1999.

Miller, Ron, and William K. Hartmann, *The Grand Tour.* New York: Workman, 1984.

Further Reading and Websites

Books

Benson, Michael. *Beyond: A Solar System Voyage.* New York: Abrams, 2009. This book is an excellent introduction to Earth's sister worlds.

Johnson, Rebecca L. *Journey into the Deep.* Minneapolis: Millbrook Press, 2011. The author travels with ocean scientists from 2000 to 2010 as they complete a census of marine life.

Kopps, Steven. *Killer Rocks from Outer Space.* Minneapolis: Twenty-First Century Books, 2004. The author describes the many objects hurtling through the galaxy.

Miller, Ron. *Mercury and Pluto.* Minneapolis: Millbrook Press, 2003. The planets that lie at the extreme limits of the solar system are subjects of this book.

——. *Venus.* Minneapolis: Millbrook Press 2002. This title is a guided tour of Earth's sister planet.

Reynolds, David. *Apollo: The Epic Journey to the Moon.* New York: Harcourt, 2002. This detailed history of human exploration of the Moon contains hundreds of photos.

Scott, Elaine. *Mars and the Search for Life.* New York: Clarion Books, 2008. Here you will find details about how scientists have been searching for signs of life on Mars.

Silverstein, Alvin, Virginia Silverstein, and Laura Silverstein Nunn. *The Universe.* Minneapolis: Twenty-First Century Books, 2009. This book explores the planets of the solar system and worlds beyond.

Websites

Astronomy
http://www.astronomy.com
This is the official website for *Astronomy* magazine.

Nine Planets
www.nineplanets.org
This website is filled with information and photos about the planets and their moons.

Sky & Telescope
http://www.skypub.com
This is the official website for *Sky & Telescope* magazine.

INDEX

ABOUT THE AUTHOR

Hugo Award–winning author and illustrator Ron Miller specializes in books about science. Among his various titles, he has written *The Elements: What You Really Want to Know*, *Special Effects: An Introduction to Movie Magic*, and *Digital Art: Painting with Pixels*. His favorite subjects are space and astronomy. A postage stamp he created is currently on board a spaceship headed for Pluto. His original paintings can be found in collections all over the world. Miller lives in Virginia.